# Sunnyboy Wants To Be A
# WEATHERMAN

By

## JAY ROSENTHAL

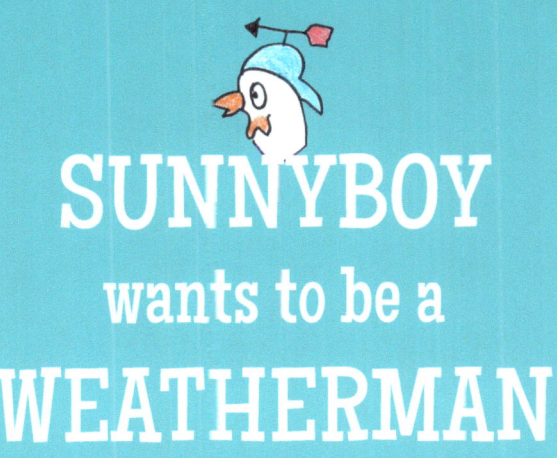

# SUNNYBOY
## wants to be a
# WEATHERMAN

A Childrens' Book

By

**JAY ROSENTHAL**

Original Illustrations by

**DANI E. HARROLD**

Art Adaptations and Color Design by

**JAY ROSENTHAL**

Design & Ideas by

**MARY KINZELBERG**

For more information about the book contact the author at AirWeather@aol.com

Dedicated to Wendy, Mike, Matt and all those
who follow their dreams, young and old.

**E**ARLY IN THE MORNING SUNNYBOY is already outside his chicken coop reading the newspaper. Now we all know that chickens are chickens, and they are not supposed to read newspapers. But here he is, looking at the Weather Page so he will know what the weather will be like and what he should wear.

His cousin, Doodle Doo shakes his wing, and cries out, "What do you think you are, Sunnyboy. A Weatherman?" Poor Sunnyboy -- he just goes around with his head in the clouds.

Sunnyboy also uses an alarm clock to get up in the morning like people do. He even takes it with him on walks. He names it 'CLOCKO'. Each night, he sets Clocko for five o'clock in the morning so he can look at the sky before the sun comes up. It makes everyone mad when it goes off and wakes them up. They cry "Sunnyboy! WHY do you have to be so DIFFERENT?"

They even wonder if Sunnyboy should leave the Coop because he is so much trouble. But the chicks cry. They don't want to *see* their big cousin Sunnyboy go away.

After he reads the weather page and knows that it will be a very hot, sunny day, Sunnyboy walks around the neighborhood, wearing light clothes, holding his yellow and red alarm clock, with the Weather Page in his back pocket. Even Clocko looks really tired in the heat. Sunnyboy notices workmen delivering ice across the street to some stores. It's lunchtime, and he sees them drop the ice on the ground, move into the shade, and pull out sandwiches to eat that have gotten warm in the heat. This gives Sunnyboy an IDEA! HE can make COLD sandwiches, and cool everyone down.

He decides to make a sandwich out of the pieces QUICKLY, before they melt in the sun. He runs across the street to the ice, stopping traffic. He picks up three pieces of ice that are flat like slices of bread. He puts one in the middle, one on the top and one on the bottom. He makes himself an ICE SANDWICH!

He thinks, 'Maybe I can take one back to the Coop before it melts and help my family cool down.' Then the surprised workmen see him. Roaring with laughter, they scratch their heads and yell, "Get away from that ice, you crazy chicken. That's OUR ice!"

He runs and takes the sandwich to the Coop but it melts of course. When word gets back to the Coop that Sunnyboy stole the ice, the family gets very upset and decides Sunnyboy now must leave, -- with Clocko.

As Sunnyboy walks sadly away, he can hear them say, ----
"Why do you have to be so different, Sunnyboy?". And you know what?
Sunnyboy really doesn't KNOW why. He's okay with being different. But he
feels very sad because he doesn't want to make the Doodle family mad at him.
He wants to make up. He wishes he could do something to make them like
him again.

Suddenly, he gets ANOTHER IDEA! (UH OH! What now?) Just ahead is an ice cream shop. He thinks that maybe if he could get everyone in the Coop an ice cream cone to cool off, they wouldn't be angry at him anymore. And then they would let him come home.

As soon as he walks into the ice cream store, the owner, Mr. Whipsomeup, says, 'Hello chicken, can I help you?'

Sunnyboy then tells him he wants to buy NINE ice cream cones, but he doesn't have any money. Mr. Whipsomeup, who is yawning from the heat, notices Sunnyboy's red and yellow alarm clock. "You know what, chicken? I wish I had an alarm clock like that so I could take a little nap until it cools down outside".

Sunnyboy responds, "I've got a great idea, Mr. Whipsomeup. I'll lend you my clock 'til tomorrow in exchange for the ice cream cones. I have inside information on the Weather and I already know tomorrow's going to be a much cooler day. And then you won't need my clock any longer". Mr. Whipsomeup says, "You sure are a smart chicken. That's a good idea!"   He takes Clocko from Sunnyboy and gives him nine cones full of yummy ice cream in return. Mr. Whipsomeup then says, "You are the first chicken customer I've ever had in here for ice cream."

Sunnyboy starts to leave the shop but before he gets out the door, he can hear Clocko yelling, PLEASE DON'T LEAVE ME! Sunnyboy looks for a moment and shouts back, DON'T WORRY, CLOCKO, I'LL BE BACK FOR YOU TOMORROW AFTER IT GETS COOLER. Eat some ice cream while you are waiting. (Clocko loves chocolate ice cream with sprinkles.)

Once Sunnyboy gets outside into the heat, he takes a quick look up at the sky to see if a lonely and puffy cumulus cloud might cover up the sun long enough to not make his ice cream melt. He heads straight home to the Coop. But because the little cloud can't cover up the whole sun, the ice cream cones soon start to melt and drip. It's EXTRA hard for him to hold all of them because chickens don't have hands like people do. Do they?! He even tries to hold one in his beak and it breaks, dripping ice cream into his nose. He looks up at the sky to see if there are any more clouds that could protect the ice cream from the sun's rays, but they are too far away to block the sun.

By the time Sunnyboy gets home to the Coop, he's a total mess. He has ice cream all over himself and his clothes. At first, the whole Doodle family laughs at him when they see him.

Chick #7, who likes fashionable clothes, comments, "I like that design on your clothes, Sunnyboy. Can you show us how to do that too?" And they all laugh some more. Then they all shout, (Group hug) "WE MISSED YOU, Sunnyboy, and you know we're GLAD you're DIFFERENT. We love you just the way you are. Even if you are a weather nut!"

Now they know that Sunnyboy is just trying to please them. Sunnyboy is so happy, he forgets all about the ice cream that is stuck on him and he shares what's left of the cones. And now he knows he can stay with the Doodle Family in the Coop.

He decides that when he gets Clocko back home again, he and Clocko will show his friends and cousins that he has what it takes to be a real weatherman. Maybe he and Clocko can do some WEATHER EXPERIMENTS together! Uh Oh!!! Here they go again. Tune in until the next story.

www.ingramcontent.com/pod-product-compliance
Lightning Source LLC
Chambersburg PA
CBHW060815290526
45792CB00005BB/1666